GOLD COAST, 2002

THANK YOU TO THE ECLECTIC PROJECTS PATRONS!

This chapbook is produced and supported by the patrons of the Eclectic Projects Fund.

Peter would like to extend his thanks to Margaret Ball, Kate Eltham, Jodi, Nicole Strickland, Meg Vann, Sally, Jennifer White, Maggie Slater, Tansy Rayner Roberts, Dave Versace; Catherine Caine, Kathleen Jennings, Stephanie Gunn, and Lois Spangler for their encouragement and support.

GOLD COAST, 2002

POEMS

PETER M. BALL

Eclectic Projects (an imprint of Brain Jar Press)
PO Box 6687
Upper Mt Gravatt, QLD, 4122
Australia
Eclectic Projects: www.PeterMBall.com
Brain Jar Press: www.BrainJarPress.com

Gold Coast 2002 Copyright © 2022 by Peter M. Ball.

The moral right of Peter M. Ball to be identified as the author of this work has been asserted.

All rights reserved. No part of this book may be reproduced in any form or by any electronic or mechanical means, including information storage and retrieval systems, without written permission from the author, except for the use of brief quotations in a book review.

Cover design by Brain Jar Press
Cover Images: Trendy abstract creative minimalist artistic hand painted composition © C Design Studio/Shutterstock.

ISBN: 978-1-922479-27-3 (Ebook) | 978-1-922479-28-0 (Chapbook)

CONTENTS

On Loan From Dreamworld I	1
Postcards	2
Gold Coast Refidex: Map 40	4
Gold Coast Connection	5
One Loan From Dreamworld II	7
Night Scenes	9
Heat Wave Dreaming	11
Aftermath	13
Indy Time	14
On Loan From Dreamworld III	16
Wolves	18
Gold Coast Refidex: Map 50	20
Surfer's Paradise Epiphany	22
Sleeping Under Neon	24
On Loan From Dreamworld IV	26
Drowning Ephemeral	28
Gold Coast Refidex: Map 70	31
Going Home Alone	33
On Loan From Dreamworld	35
Johnson St, Southport, 9:27 PM	36
Gold Coast Refidex: Map 29	39
Jadran Motel	41
On Loan From Dreamworld V	44
Gold Coast Refidex: Map 60	46
About the Author	47

ON LOAN FROM DREAMWORLD I

This city produces cafes, lattes, focaccia, frescos, Tuscan design, bad prints of famous paintings

This city produces cafes, coffees, ambience, Tekno, Portishead, Macy Gray and an overworked interior decorator

This city produces cafes, cakes, rolls, beachfronts, bare feet, salt air, sand, towels and bad cappuccino

This city produces falling trees, filled in mangroves, the crushing weight of multi-million international hotel resorts

This city produces statues of our heroes, military and life-saver, lining the boardwalk of Surfers Paradise in the warm summer nights

This city produces bad soapies, American movies, made for TV, no art, no theatre, no writing, no drawing or dreaming

This city produces world competition surfers, lifesavers, crashing through white wash with broad, bronze chests

This city almost produced Baywatch, but someone changed their mind

POSTCARDS

1.

    Palm trees in concrete
    held together with fairy lights
    spaced for the view
    placed for the shade
    if you look close
    some of them
    even seem real

2.

    Whatever you want, you know we've got
    the Wipe-out, The Big Drop, The Lethal Weapon
    Pacific Fair, Australia Fair, Billabong, Rusty
    Friday night Markets on Paradise Beach
    Indy cars, Pit stops, Nightclubs, Sand
    The collective desire of a two week holiday

3.

    Back seat of a taxi
    the driver knows: new-wave
    French critical theory, a po-mo
    deconstruction of Australian literature,
    and exactly how far
    its all are going to get him

4.

    6:50 AM, time to leave. So I take
    a ten minute walk to
    Broadwater McDonalds: $3.25 McMuffin
    $1.20 for coffee
    My day's not worth starting any better
    When all the city asks
    is that I keep out of the way

5.

    Just a short drive away
    an escape from streets and skyline
    green, native trees, air scented with earth
    the cool retreat of hinterland
    nature's beauty waiting
    for those who need a day's relief

GOLD COAST REFIDEX: MAP 40

Surfers Paradise, Broadbeach, Chevron Island
I lived here once, crashing in hallways
after big nights on the town, drinking
smoking, sleeping in my clothes, on carpet
One guy lived there, twelve of us infested
paying our rent in pizza, vodka, iced coffee, pot

Chevron Island drained brain and spirit
guzzled it down to the chorus of scol, scol, scol, scol
Sleep was always dreamless, waking the same
time warped and folded like an origami bird
some of us moved on, too fast,
or, perhaps, too slow

we grew up
gave up
left the rest to decompose

GOLD COAST CONNECTION

A thousand feet and lowering

blue sky
blue sea
tarmac

WELCOME TO THE GOLD COAST
This is Paradise

Collect your luggage and step out
into sweltering heat, your sweat
prickling your thighs. A disappointing
first view of the skyline—there's nothing
over five stories

Find your shuttle bus: small,
cramped, white. This is your
Gold Coast Con-X-ion
between airport, hotel, theme park

The driver's name is Ray: young
tanned, sunscreen scent, his mirrored
sunglasses reflect your face back at you.

He loads you. Your bags. The other passengers
Drives down the highway

You're headed for Surfers: forty minutes drive
down a highway artery with
small town ambience

Ray tells you it's a good day
takes you past Burleigh Beach
In the distance, you see
your first Gold Coast wave
rising up, breaking
like the promise of heaven

Ray talks about the city
pointing, teeth in the rear-view
fingers jab, a barrage of landmarks
Beaches, Buildings, Signs Streets, Palm trees, Life savers,
    Beaches, Cavill Ave.
Towers, now. The holiday skyline. Buildings stretch like
    fingers clawing at a slice of sky

Ray drives onward, blasé
He's seen the fingers a hundred times, so he concentrates
follows the lines of the palm.

The Con-X-ion connects
lobby, five star hotel/resort
check in manned by teenage girls dressed in girl scout
    uniforms, matching red ties, no flaws

A blond girl greets you and takes money, smiles.
Even her teeth are perfect.

You're handed the keys, someone takes your luggage
So you follow them, fourteen stories up, to your place
high in the Paradise sky

ONE LOAN FROM DREAMWORLD II

This city produces nightclubs, bouncers, cocktails, boob tubes, high heels, tight shirts, surf boards, neon and hangovers

This city produces twenty-firsts, retirement parties, eighteenths, lost loves and hopeless romances

This city produces strip clubs, nudity, fantasy, sex, lap dances, g-strings, hormonal escapes

This city produces a market for Panadol, Tylenol, alcohol, no-doze and Berocca

This city produces smoky nights, bleary eyes, dirty porcelain, shooters, shakers, slammers, everything that makes the perfect night out

This city produces 12" pizza, doner kebab, McDonald's burgers, Hungry Jacks, KFC, added preservatives and junkies

This city produces Hard Rock, Shooters, Cocktails, MP's, Rosies, Billy's, Fever, Fortunes and the Edge

This city produces experiences with the drunk, the stoned, the speeding, the angry, the lost, the temporary and the beach

This city produces thick congested highway arteries clogged with people coming and people running out

This city produces empty beach front horizon lines
    devoid of ocean traffic

This city produces the image of sex
sand
sex on sand
an early morning surf

NIGHT SCENES

5:49 PM

> Night falls
> Cocktails & Dreams
> light up
> a neon *o* burns out
> so do you
> You dream/become
> a black dot in the heart
> (the city has none)
>
> Night falls
> God/Paradise
> Surfer/Jesus
> They don't want you as a sunbeam anymore,

10:15 PM

> No dreams found here, drowning in a bottle of Southern Comfort. A stranger here, a dark club, lit by flashing strobes.
> (You've been here before, maybe)

Kids/pick/labels/drink/
drug/tablet/liquid/needle
VB/MDMA/LSD/UDL
cocaine/amphetamine
You don't belong (but no-one does).

3:00 AM

Centre line, Pacific Highway, biding time
Waiting for Rolls Royce/BMW
Mazerati/Ferrari/Porsche Embrace
You listen
the ghosts of cars.

4:20 AM

Day comes early
sunglasses/bleary eyes
you've made yourself empty
ain't that just a scream

you can hear, echoing, up there
bouncing off high-rise balconies

HEAT WAVE DREAMING

Gold Coast, early AM
writing poetry in bed
while a storm brews
above the grey-tile rooftop

Tonight, all there is
is thirty degree heat
high humidity, warm sweat

Sweat pooling in fake leather seats
in the bath, in the bed
in the belly-button
of the brown eyed girl
creating rivers and dams
waterfalls in her body

Tonight, sleep is absent
but dreaming and I
are old comrades in arms
whispering in each others ear
about our eventual escape

About stealing ourselves

a beamer, a volvo, a limo
anything, cranking the air-con
and running like hell

Dreaming and heat
go hand in hand for me
with sweat comes the need
to find a place to escape
to go some place cold
where the pure, white snow
makes my hands go numb

Tonight, all I desire
is to steal the hand
of the brown-eyed girl
and run, escape, fly
anything to leave behind
the heat and the dreams
that are driving me crazy

Outside the storm brews
the heat continues
the brown eyed girl sleeps

I lie back in sweat

AFTERMATH

It's 1 AM on a Sunday morning
I'm throwing up: cheap wine
beer
pizza
Macdonald's burgers
French fries
a medium Coke
and what little remains of my dignity

INDY TIME

Leave Harry's Surfer's apartment
eight PM, the racing's done

Holden won
(for today, anyway)

Flash an orange wrist pass
so the steroid-enhanced security monsters
nod in recognition.
I'm ID'd: Friend, visiting a friend,
now trying to get away

The air stinks
petrol hormones adrenalin
the Ford guys sulk
Holden guys gloat
The rest of us try to get home

I'm bailed up in a side street
strong hands on throat
fists in gut
the taste of vomit
a knee in the groin

Adrenaline renders it all in details:
A flash of flannel
Blood shot eyes
Petrol fumes and bad hair
voice like a V8's snarl
Ford or Holden?
Dunno. Guess fast
Ford?
Hands melt away. Flannel leaves
I breath free
Feeling lucky

Girls wander past, feigning ignorance
Peroxide, fake tan, gold bikini,
& a Metre Maid's red sash
Accent pegs them: tourist chicks on the prowl,
Not the real deal.

So many guys drunk on petrol,
adrenaline, and beer.
They don't notice
the absence the words on the sash
'til the messy haze of morning.

I retreat to the suburbs, to other friends
I can visit without tickets, armbands
the cars become hidden monsters.

A week spent
sitting on balconies, smoking
sipping red cordial or beer.
Listening to the growl of invisible engines
charging along the wind.
We grin and scare one another:
Don't go to Surfer's man
The Indy might get you

ON LOAN FROM DREAMWORLD III

This city produces a sixteen year old semi-goth reformed junk hiding out in the wilderness with pot and solitude
This city produces eight year old delinquents threatening sexual abuse in the schoolyard to get back at forty year old delinquent parents
This city produces teenage kids being moved on in shopping centres because a teenage kid with three friends is a gang
This city produces film makers, artists, poets, novelists, actors, and then makes them want to leave
This city produces a fear of the young

This city produces barefoot ferals with dole cheques, dreadlocks, dance raves, trance, ambient, vegan, doof, doof, doof into early dawn
This city produces bare-chested surfers, long hair and board shorts, up with the tides and following the karma of the ocean
This city produces alcos and stoners, nothing to live for but the hope of a cheap escape
This city produces mobile phone yuppies hoarding

money and living in the air with the wind and the
sunrise

This city produces few people
it prefers to import them

WOLVES

In the distance
there's the howl of wolves
lying under headlights on the Spit
prowling under the Southport street lamps
Taking secret drinks in Surfer's gutters
and suburban bars
noses straining under harsh illumination
sniffing for something they can't find

Flickering between light and shadow
they move on, drifting past on bikes
boards, blades, the soft pad
of paws on bitumen barely heard
felt, if it's noticed at all
Behind closed windows
we hide like pigs
in a house of straw

Wolves
lurking out there, invisible
grey flickers, voiceless shadows

almost seen, never heard

except from a distance
the howl of wolves

cutting through the darkness
sad
alone

GOLD COAST REFIDEX: MAP 50

Mermaid Beach and Miami
I lived here twice:

Once in a garage bedroom
underneath a friend's parents' house
no rent, $50 board, forget to pay
stare at concrete walls at night
walk the beachfront, take the dog
stand on cliffs and watch the moon
turn the water into liquid mercury

Once on three friends' couch, Magic Mountain
a former theme park remade a resort
there were two strippers, one student
I'd crash four, five nights a week
hang out, hand outs, not eating, driving
late night work pick ups, parties, shopping trips

Sitting on balconies, bored and dreaming
drinking coffee or beer, I'd watch
the signs, Miami High School's
HI MIAMI HIGH

Rhema Church, purple neon cross
next to yellow twenty-four hour
Shell servo your one-stop shop
coke, cigarettes, fuel and faith

SURFER'S PARADISE EPIPHANY

I talk to God, standing
on the corner of Cavill and Orchid
basking in the sunset reflected and refracted
off a thousand upon a thousand
high rise windows, balconies, tourist sunglasses
heard and repeated
by bewildered listeners drinking XXXX
watching the surf from their penthouses
twenty-five stories in the sky

I talk to God, my voice echoing in heaven
I doubt he listens, or that he's interested
From his vantage point, we who are grounded
must seem ugly and poor compared to those
who live with him in the high-rise sky
paying the $400 a week rent
that keeps his world going round
From his vantage point, I'm probably just
another crazy fucker in a city full of madness
my voice drowning in the sound of surf

I talk to God, standing beside the house of law
screaming from the shadows of a concrete Eden

all I want is absolution from a city
that craves only enough height to spit from

I'm like half the people who live here
empty wallets, empty pasts, empty souls
craving the height of heaven and the voice
that speaks through bank accounts and assets
mortgaging its own place in the sky

SLEEPING UNDER NEON

Sleeples, curtain, crack: neon
Hotel vacant
Lit neon means (no) vacancy

Tonight, I sleep under neon
Neon means sleeping means party means booze
Neon means nudity/sex/promise/death
Cheap wine/bourbon/hazy memories
Sleepless, again.

Neon means star/burn/trapped/glass/tube
Coastline children/Neon births
Neon children/birthed by tube
Neon children/burn
Burning children, no sleep.

We trapped the stars in neon.

Gold Coast, I sleep under neon for you.
A child, burning.

I sleep, child of dreaming coastline
My first memory: neon

My first thought: neon
My dreams: neon, coastline, darkness.

Spotlight/bar: neon
Breast/body/cunt
face/neon/faceless

Neon means: nudity/sex/promise
Neon means: faceless/promise/death
Neon means: faceless/sex

Gold Coast, home to faceless children
Features scoured by neon.

Sleep/alone/neon/crack
Fight/neon/sleep/sleep
Dream/neon/coastline/dreaming

The view from my bed: curtains, window, neon.
Red/neon; blue/neon; green/neon.
Faceless/neon
Sleep/under/sex/promise/faceless/neon
Sleep/dream: neon

Gold Coast, I sleep under neon for you, and my dreams
burn like trapped stars, unable
to break free.

ON LOAN FROM DREAMWORLD IV

This city produces bad body image, an adherence to clone wear, and an embarrassment of beautiful people
This city produces facial scars from drunken brawls with guys who hated you in high school
This city produces cosmetic surgery, growing breasts, swelling cocks, smaller noses, thinner thighs and plastic populations
This city produces middle-aged women with varicose veins and long pants hiding in the suburbs
This city produces middle-aged women with linen suits and money flaunting their himbo toy boys
This city produces male divorcees with young models, newlyweds with new-made dreams, retired couples with ignored lives and single people hunting in the wrong hunting grounds
This city produces fear of the young, fear of the poor, fear of the dark and fear of the old
This city produces dirty weekends, one-night stands, drunken pick-ups, morning-after regrets and the anniversary holiday

This city produces high rise paranoia, voyeurism, who's

watching who, unlit balcony windows—keep your
blinds drawn, asshole

DROWNING EPHEMERAL

Five after Midnight
we gave in
decided it was time
to drift home

We were thrown out
of Rosies, Shooters, the Party
we found no-one and nothing
amongst the neon, the starlight
the spirit of Rock'n'Roll

Floating past the Hard Rock
electric brown guitar
whisky flavoured nostalgia
we wonder if this city
ever had a soul

Floating past the Night Owl
twenty four hours
soft-drink and porn
we wonder where this city
keeps its lost ghosts
Floating past the Pink Poodle

glowing pink guard dog
watching over the roadside
we wonder where this city
keeps its local stories

Under the shifting lights of Jupiters
Five lights rolling
down the sloped casino roof
we parted ways
half-drunk, lost, wandering toward home

The city's current pulled me southwards
Through Broadbeach
Cafe society at its most oblivious
Through Nobby's Beach
The Tuscan fortress/apartments of Magic Mountain
Through Burleigh Heads
The park at twilight filled with lorikeet chatter

The city pulled me south
past white crosses
picketed into the earth
Jamie's friend Alex
crossing at the wrong place
after the time of his life

Past houses I used to know
beat up and windows broken
needle marks
up a tanned coast arm

Past a bridge
views of forested hills, expensive homes
Currumbin beachfront from the railing
my friend Brian tried to fly here
He knew that he couldn't

Southwards
as far south as I know in this city
lying on a hilltop
watching rolling beach, mangroves
the electronic lighthouse
beaming radio waves instead of light

Daylight isn't far off
the skyline will turn red in an hour

the sun will come to greet this tourist city
for another day

It's my five thousand
one hundred and thirteenth morning
spent in this city

It's an old friend
leaving at daylight

GOLD COAST REFIDEX: MAP 70

Currumbin, Elanora, Palm Beach
I lived here once, three bedroom
brick house, pool and study, no rent

I spent hours wandering canals
back paths filled with pine trees
walked three kilometres to a beach
with rock walls, pale yellow sand
more locals there than tourists

I sipped coffee with school friends
The Moontide Cafe, The Balcona Lounge
both quiet, empty, removed
like the suburbs, close enough
to the beachfront to smell salt

I first swam in the ocean here
age six, boogie boarding, scared
red swimmers over scrawny flesh
memories of Jaws still in my head

Currumbin, Elanora, Palm Beach

the pulse so slow it barely beats
I lived three K's inland
shhh
you can almost hear waves

GOING HOME ALONE

The bus shifts a gear
roars down the Gold Coast highway
interior lit by fluorescent light

I stare at my reflection in the window
catch sight of the old couple
bus riding at 1 AM, Sunday morning
Leaning close, hands held, talking

I find myself trying to make out the words
they're hiding amongst their murmur
desperate to know
what they're saying to each other
The way they hold each other
heads close and bodies locking
the way they whisper and murmur together
they way they love each other
like two people who know each other

This old couple gives the appearance
of being together for a long time

It's a lifeline I can't comprehend

getting together in your twenties
dying together in your eighties
Staying together for sixty years
bus rides with single teenagers
filling your autumn years

We're only two generations apart
this old couple together and me all alone
but across the aisle separating us
age stretches like a gorge

ON LOAN FROM DREAMWORLD

This city produces expensive buses that cling to the coast-
line with asshole drivers who hate anyone who can't
afford a car
This city produces a high cost, independent gallery selling
Brett Whitely, Charles Blackman, Aussie painters,
Overseas investors, 40% commission, sir please leave
and get some shoes
This city produces a mad Red Baron stunt pilot giving
tourists a bird's eye view over Gold Coast, loop the
loop then go home to middle-aged wife, two kids,
night job of father, husband, name of Joseph

This city produces glamour
your next door neighbour
a movie star
on holidays

JOHNSON ST, SOUTHPORT, 9:27 PM

Under streetlight
starlight
grey moths and bats
we walk

Past the half-formed husks
of growing townhouse/units
Past the black front
of the abandoned corner store
Past the quiet faces
of houses sleeping

This place is dormant
between the hours of nine and breakfast

Arm in arm we walk
curious
about random-scatter
room lights peeking out
behind half-drawn blinds

To pass the time
we theorise:

See there
Someone's fucking in there
Some no-frills husband
generic brand wife
making time
for themselves
while the kids sleep

See there
that's a granny flat
one-bedroom
one lonely guy
passed out on the floor
60 watts burning

See there
that's the house of young guys
doleys, new start
first start really
settling in, three days before payday
Buffy, Dawsons, Ally McBeal
the best of mid-week programming
while they wait out
the absence of VB

We each cast three shadows on the bitumen
count the stars past the streetlights
The houses don't give much away
but you can guess what they're hiding

The street prefers silence
this time of night
nothing to hear but the slow beating
of the suburban heart

The air's clear tonight
no petrochemical aftertaste

the sound of the surf
drifts in
from the other side of the Broadwater

Tonight, we walk Johnson together
Arm in arm
through the veins of suburbia

GOLD COAST REFIDEX: MAP 29

Southport, Main Beach, Labrador
I lived here once, hiding out
in a highway hotel, unhappy
$125 a week, no food, no hope
I lived like a stray dog, skulking
dreaming of somewhere better
walking the park by the Broadwater
staring at Seaworld lights
across the river mouth, shining
gleaming like hope and promise

Southport, I live here now
3 bedrooms, double story
$220 a week, quiet street, sharing
sitting on the balcony
watching mountains shaded green
rising up behind suburbs

Maps 28, 29, 30, 37
Arundel, Parkwood, Ashmore
Benowa, Nerang, Carrara
one story houses, homes

people
pulling their pants on one leg at a time
getting married, going out, having kids
living out their lives day
after day

JADRAN MOTEL

Out of the way, aging
the haven for me
& others

Living on my left—the old women
black leather pants, white leather face
a lesbian living large
With her slightly younger...Son? Husband? Friend?

Living on my right, the Maori family
going out, doors slamming, 11 PM or 1 AM.

Above me, the invisible family
footsteps, toilets, running, screaming
the sounds of fists, flesh
hitting the floor (we should call the cops)

I learned to live life without
television, stereo, creature comforts.
Couches, a bed, cigarettes, and food.

I learned to keep my head down
my eyes & ears closed

Hello?
...
Hello? This is a call
Hello? This city
it's moving

growing surfing
building flowing
driving fucking

collap/
sing

Can you hear me?
This city? It's collapsing

At night
I sit on my balcony
white flesh stucco walls
bathed in florescent green glow
rising up under the low rail
fuck knows why
drink cheap wine
plastic cups
watch the cars drive
Gold Coast Highway

Ford Holden Holden Bike Beamer Ford Mazda Limo
    Limo Holden Limo Bike Ford Holden Empty Empty
    Empty Empty Empty

About midnight
the traffic stops
the glow blinks out
I sleep

This can't last forever

The giant boxes, the people
Awake/Asleep; Irrelevant
the people dream

I dream

Can you hear me?
This city moves.
This city dreams.

Dawn comes
as always

I go to work
looking for work

Wanted:Casual junior — Office Work, Promotions
Wanted:Casual junior — Weekend work, Food prep
Wanted:Holiday only — Themeworld, Character actor
Wanted:Casual Junior — McDonalds, Dayshift
Wanted:Attractive Girls — Young, Make $600 a day

Me: 23, Male. Qualified to
Think. Dream. Flail.
Fail.

I go to work
Hand in form
Dream

Return to white stucco walls

ON LOAN FROM DREAMWORLD V

This city produces laws against teenage car engine stereos loud music infringing on the sacred site of tourists everywhere
This city produces fewer and fewer places for the young and lower class to go, but more and more places for them to hide
This city produces dreams, dreams, dreams, dreams that come and go like the tides and the waves
This city produces cliff top sunrise over ocean on a clear morning that hurts the eyes,
makes you cry and believe the city is beautiful

This city produces mid-life crisis, bald heads, sportscars, surfboards, surf skis, marijuana haze, model girlfriends, lost youth, short term gratification
This city produces perfect bodies, brown skin, fashion nazis, tight shirts, bikini tops, mini skirts, board shorts
This city produces penthouse apartments floating on three thousand lives and shifting sand
This city produces neon, nightclubs, postcards, beach fronts, tides, tubes, titillation

This city produces a fascination
with bared breasts
other people's money

GOLD COAST REFIDEX: MAP 60

Burleigh Heads, Burleigh Waters, Stephens, Andrews
I lived here once, in a two bedroom, second story
apartment in beachfront holiday flats, no rent needed
I shared the smaller bedroom with my younger sister

We travelled a half-hour south for school back then
we'd come home and sprint the driveway and stairs
scared of the hulking cranes with flashing lights
building the highrise next door would drop concrete
 blocks
at night I had bad dreams, the sky was always falling

Burleigh Heads, beachfront, thin parks, road, units
after my family moved, I'd come back years later
visit friends with beer and pot, get drunk, high
walk in groups along the beachfront and parks
under silver moon on the beach sands, lights in
accompanying parks and shadows on the forest
covered hills, finish early, go to the Fish Hut
the best chips you can get on the Gold Coast

ABOUT THE AUTHOR

PETER M. BALL is an author, publisher, and RPG gamer whose love of speculative fiction emerged after exposure to *The Hobbit*, *Star Wars*, David Lynch's *Dune*, and far too many games of *Dungeons and Dragons* before the age of 7. He's spent the bulk of his life working as a creative writing tutor, with brief stints as a performance poet, gaming convention organiser, online content developer, non-profit arts manager, GenreCon convenor, and d20 RPG publisher.

He's the author of the Miriam Aster series and the Keith Murphy Urban Fantasy Thrillers, three short story collections, and more stories, articles, poems, and RPG material than he'd care to count.

He's the brain-in-charge at Brain Jar Press, an aspiring made scientist running publishing experiments through Eclectic Projects, and resides in Brisbane, Australia, with his partner and a very affectionate cat.

Find Peter Online at PeterMBall.com *or reach out to Peter on your favourite Social Media platforms:*

- facebook.com/PeterMBall
- twitter.com/PeterMBall
- instagram.com/PeterMBall
- goodreads.com/PeterMBall
- patreon.com/PeterMBall

ALSO BY PETER M. BALL

SHORT STORY COLLECTIONS

The Birdcage Heart & Other Strange Tales

Not Quite The End Of the World Just Yet: Short Stories & Strange Futures

These Strange & Magic Things: Short Stories

MIRIAM ASTER NOVELLAS

Horn

Bleed

BRAIN JAR PRESS SHORT FICTION LAB

The Early Experiments

Winged, With Sharp Teeth

8 Minutes Of Usable Daylight

A White Cross Beside A Lonely Road

One Last First Date Before The End Of The World

Shedding Skins

ESSAYS

You Don't Want To Be Published & Other Things Nobody Tells You When You First Start Writing

THANK YOU FOR BUYING THIS ECLECTIC PROJECTS CHAPBOOK

To receive special offers, bonus content, and info on new releases and other great reads, sign up for our newsletters.

To get more from the author, Peter M. Ball, you can sign up for his newsletter at PeterMBall.com

www.ingramcontent.com/pod-product-compliance
Lightning Source LLC
Chambersburg PA
CBHW021452080526
44588CB00009B/820